W9-CFE-277

Book 6

I Like the ABCs

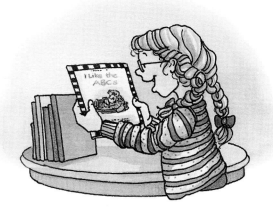

by Francie Alexander

Illustrated by Maxie Chambliss

SCHOLASTIC

A B C D

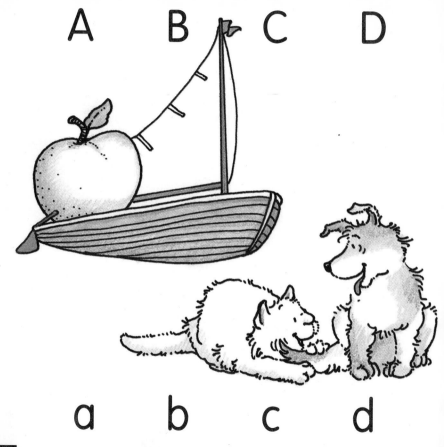

a b c d

2

E F G H

e f g h

3

I J K L M

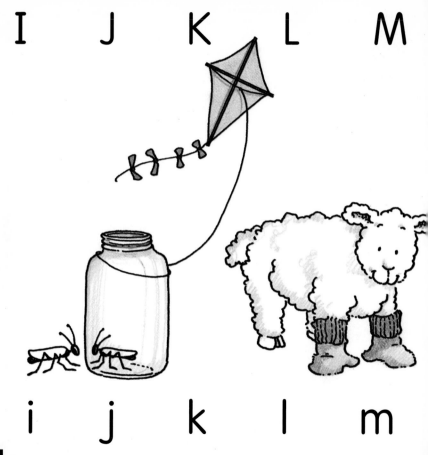

i j k l m

4

N O P Q R

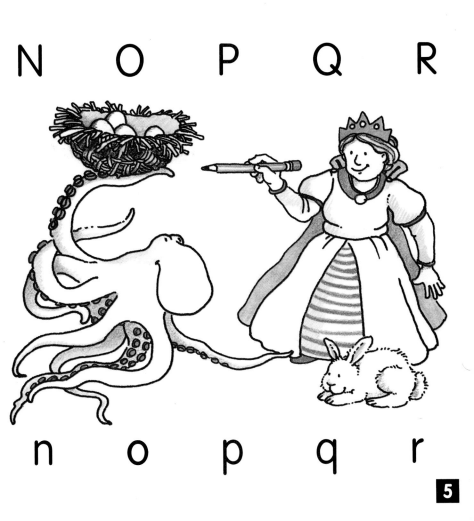

n o p q r

5

S T U V W

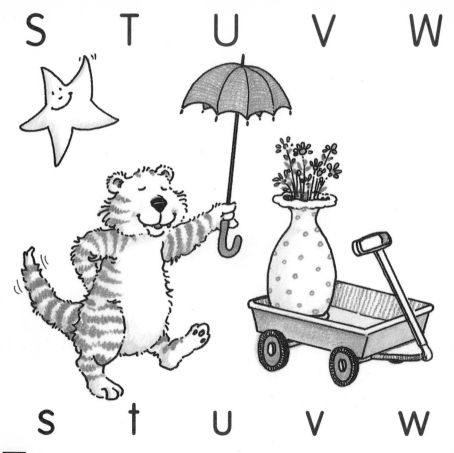

S t u v W

6

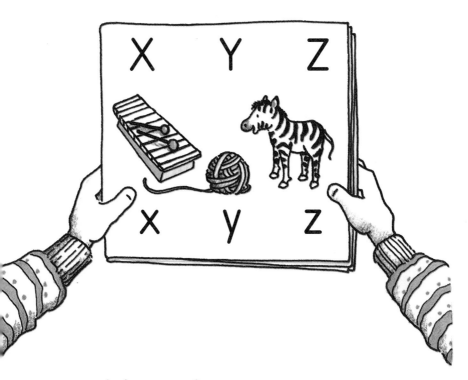

I like the ABCs!

My Words

*like

*new high frequency words